HAPPY
—HOLIDAYS—

Relax by Rail

THE GOLDEN AGE OF RAILWAY POSTERS

INTRODUCED BY MICHAEL PALIN

PAVILION

This edition published in 1998 by
PAVILION BOOKS LIMITED
London House, Great Eastern Wharf,
Parkgate Road, London SW11 4NQ

First published in Great Britain in 1987 by
Pavilion Books Limited

Text © Michael Palin 1987
Posters © The British Railways Board and The Tindale
Collection 1987

Posters supplied by Avon Anglia

Designed by Peter Bridgewater Associates
Associate Editor: Russell Ash

British Library Cataloguing in Publication Data
Happy holidays: the golden age of
railway posters.
1. Resorts—Posters   2. Posters, British
769'.436   NC1849.H43

2 4 6 8 10 9 7 5 3 1

ISBN 1 86205 189 5

Printed and bound in Singapore by Kyodo

*The publisher would like to thank the following for providing
pictures for this book:*
The BBC Hulton Picture Library: 7 (top and bottom, right), 9
(bottom right), 12, 13; British Rail 2, 6, 10, 11 (top, left and right), 14,
15, 46, 80; The National Railway Museum: 1, 4, 8, 11 (bottom left),
16, 20, 24, 26, 28, 30, 32, 34, 36, 38, 40, 42, 50, 56, 60, 62, 70, 72,
76, 82, 84, 88, 92, 94; Topham: 7 (top left), 9 (top right).

CONTENTS

*The posters are arranged to make a sweeping tour of the
United Kingdom, starting in London and then working
clockwise around many of the popular holiday resorts. They
are listed alphabetically here for ease of reference.*

I F ever I should be asked to close my eyes and think of England (and I'm always hopeful) I feel sure that I would come up with a railway poster. Probably of the period between 1930 and 1950, and probably painted by Claude Buckle or Frank Mason, Ronald Lampitt or Jack Merriott, Tom Purvis, Sydney Lee, or any one of the names as solid and dependable as the hills, dales, coastlines and cathedrals they once so skilfully depicted. Outrageously selective their vision of our septic isle may have been, there is, nevertheless, something undeniably reassuring and comforting about the world of uncomplicated pleasure and unalloyed beauty which they defined. It is a timeless world in which skies are always partly cloudy, suggesting moderation and temperance. The weather is as British as briar pipes and grey flannel trousers, a little dull perhaps but never dangerous. The countryside, carefully preserved by this equable climate, echoes its harmony. Hills and valleys are green and well watered, landscapes are delightfully proportioned and quite free from any stain

of progress. Whenever humans are depicted, which is not that often, they too are delightfully proportioned. Harmonious heterosexual couples with 1.5 children. The men are slim, angular Biggles clones, the women generally pert and wholesome. It's a Utopia, a Britain on which partly cloudy skies never set and in which the Industrial Revolution never happened; a jigsaw-puzzle world from which strife and ill health are absent, where everyone smiles and no one coughs or cheats. It's Happy Valley, and it's yours for the price of a day return. But there's the irony. As you look more closely one significant element seems to be missing from this poster Paradise, and that is the railway train. The railway train can be noisy and dirty. It rattles and clanks and whistles and hisses and belches out smoke. Steel and brass and grease and coal and oil and fire have no place in this Arcadian idyll, and yet, without the railway train it would never have had to be created. The awkward relationship between the beauty of Britain and one of its defilers is what this book is all about.

The rich collection of posters gathered here mirrors the railways' image from 1930s optimism to 1950s nostalgia. To anyone who travelled in that period they bring back memories. I had an LMS poster of Shrewsbury on my wall at home for a full three years before I went to school there. They were part of a world which included those lugubrious sepia panels in railway compartments, of which one in particular, that of Mother Shipton's Well at Knaresborough, was so disturbing I had to spend most of the journey in the

Go West, young man! (and woman): Francis A. Beck's simple evocation of the joys of rail tours.

Lacking the stylish appeal of Antibes or Rio, perhaps, but this Sheringham luggage label conjures nostalgic associations of its own.

Whitsun at Waterloo: the queue for the Isle of Wight train, 8 June 1957.

race up to the guard's van at every change, to make sure his bike hadn't been off-loaded for Mablethorpe or Hunstanton. My parents must have gone through hell to get us all to Sheringham. No wonder they needed two weeks' holiday at the end of it. But their anxiety never affected my excitement, which built throughout the day until, with the sun by now declining, we pulled away from Melton Constable and I knew that soon I would be seeing the sea for the first time in 50 weeks.

In the nineteenth century the railway had virtually created holiday resorts. After the railway arrived in Brighton in 1841, the population rose by nearly 20,000 in ten years. One week in 1859 73,000 people travelled by train to the resort. Bournemouth, on the other hand, resisted the railway's corrupting influence until 1870, but in the next ten years its population rose from 5,000 to 17,000. But by the 1920s the railways no longer had the

corridor. I remember too, holidays by rail – embarking on the long haul from Sheffield to Sheringham, a journey which involved about 37 changes, but which I found as exciting as a thriller film in its slow buildup to the sea. The excitement began three or four days before we left, for our buckets, spades, water-wings and athlete's foot powder had to be packed early, in heavy leather suitcases stamped with the magic letters PLA – Passenger's Luggage In Advance. I dimly remember a snub-nosed articulated vehicle arriving outside the house and my shout from the window 'Pickford's is here!' which meant the holiday had begun. Then, at approximately 7.27 on the morning of the great day of departure, a large shiny Austin with a running board of prodigious width drew up in the road. I was always the first to see it, but then I'd been looking out for it for almost an hour. This was Mr Lambert's taxi. It probably also doubled as a hearse, for we drove to Sheffield Victoria station with a heart-thumping lack of urgency. There my father, who had arrived earlier to get his bicycle on the train, was waiting. He was getting very twitchy, and had already visited the toilets.

The journey began behind a softly clanking Class B1 – an unassuming middle-range locomotive named incongruously after obscure African wild animals. (61027 was 'Modoqua', and 61035, which, to my eternal regret, I never saw, was called 'Pronghorn'.) Train-spotting possibilities waned as we slipped into the quiet branch lines of Lincolnshire, and the day wore on slowly as we were deposited at a variety of increasingly unlikely stations and halts. I have dim memories of my father having to

Summer holidays by rail, 1920s-style:
Top: the whole family sets forth at Paddington.
Bottom: waiting at Victoria.

A bold poster from the earliest established holiday company, Thomas Cook, who had been arranging rail tours since 1841.

The symbiotic relationship between railways and holidays began with the excursion. The first of these is generally held to have been in 1841, when Thomas Cook organised trains to take a thousand Methodists to Nottingham for a temperance rally. The first seaside excursion, according to Anthony Hern's book *The Seaside Holiday*, was run in 1843 on the initiative of Sir Rowland Hill, inventor of the penny post. Up till this time the attractions of railway travel had been pitched toward a wealthy and exclusive market. Mass travel was not considered a laudable goal.

But the potential of specials and excursions gradually opened up a market – for organised groups, for employers like the Lancashire boss who, in 1844, took 650 of his workers to Fleetwood for the day, and for anyone needing to escape from the increasingly smoky, built-up, industrial areas for a breath of fresh air. The railway companies came down off their high horses, and third class travel, special fares and bargains began to be

Up to the north for the Easter holidays: an enterprising promotion for some early rail excursions via the Great Northern Railway.

resorts to themselves. In 1922 the first Austin Seven was produced and the age of mass motoring had begun. The following year, too, was a significant one for the railways. In 1923 the plethora of small railway companies which had existed before the First World War were grouped into four new companies, the LNER, the LMS, the Great Western and the Southern Railway. To announce their presence and flex their new-found muscle the companies all embarked on big publicity campaigns. The LNER commissioned top graphic artists for a series of 34 new posters in two years. The LMS used Royal Academicians like Augustus John and Sir William Orpen, but the Great Western and Southern were less sophisticated. They continued to work closely with the resorts in the production of their publicity, often to the detriment of the artist who was forced to tailor his work to the whim of the town council, and this may account for why much of the holiday poster work was safe and reassuring compared to the bold experiments being carried out by the LNER and LMS.

announced from handbills and posters. In 1846 'Carlisle Races and Wrestling' could be enjoyed for five shillings, third class return from Newcastle, and in 1851 the Great Exhibition attracted six million visitors, the majority of them carried by train. An 1864 MNE poster announced a special from York to the Garibaldi Demonstration at Crystal Palace for ten shillings and sixpence return, and the International Poultry and Pigeon show merited a South-East and Chatham Special.

In 1871 the first Bank Holiday was instituted, consolidating the mass movement from industrial centres to the coast, and quiet little communities like Margate and Eastbourne and Blackpool found themselves in demand as the discovery of the seaside with its abundant supply of life-enhancing ozone began. With it came the annual summer migration 'when England leaves her centre for her tide-line' as John Betjeman described it in his poem 'Beside the Seaside'.

Holiday posters to stimulate this market began to emerge in the late nineteenth century. In 1908 perhaps the most famous railway poster of all was produced by the Great Northern Railway. It was drawn by John Hassall and depicted a jolly prancing fisherman and the immortal legend 'Skegness is SO bracing'. But such whimsicality was the exception rather than the rule and for the most part Edwardian and Victorian posters were restrained and factual. Whilst the French were hinting at all sorts of exotic encounters in the railway posters of the *belle epoque*, British railway companies remained steadfastly pipe-in-mouth. North east England was extolled as 'The Golfer's Elysium'. Railway hotels offered 'Tranquil Solitude' and 'Extensive Sands', whilst in commercial terms 'Southport for Mild Winters' sounded suicidally inoffensive. However, the Great Western Railway pulled an admirably creative fast one in 1908 when some bored office worker discovered that if you turned Cornwall round by 90 degrees it bore a passing resemblance to a much-visited European country. This was duly graphically represented, accompanied by one of history's longest and most dubious slogans 'There Is A Great Similarity between Cornwall and Italy in Shape, Climate and Natural Beauties'. Whether people re-booked from Perugia to Padstow or Naples to Newquay is not recorded.

After the First World War, the newly reformed railways set out to sell themselves in a variety of ways. Special low fares were introduced, there were 'Save To Travel' schemes and all sorts of Day Trip bargains. There were link-ups with the growing motor coach and charabanc services – many of them owned by the railways themselves. The GWR introduced catering

Waiting at Waterloo: Top: August Bank Holiday, 1947. Bottom: the compleat cyclist and companion.

baskets and there were intimations of the fast food world to come when they opened a Quick Lunch Bar at Paddington. Catering again for the snack-bar rather than restaurant car market the LNER introduced 'Buffet Expresses' in 1932, the GWR brought in 'café-cars' and in 1938 the Southern Railway introduced a ten-stool travelling bar. The LMS pioneered open saloon layouts to accommodate more third class ticket holders, but the GWR disapproved of such informality and refused to use open-plan on scheduled services. Despite the Depression it was a buyer's market as the 1930s wore on and jigsaw puzzles, picture postcards and even on-train hairdressing and cinema facilities were all tried out in order to win passengers. To add a little glamour to their services the companies began to increase the number of named trains. The holiday-maker from the midlands and north was lured to Bournemouth by the evocatively titled 'Pines Express', the south Cornish coast was officially declared to be a Riviera by the 'Cornish Riviera Limited' and the Southern railway went for quality, introducing no less than four named Pullman Services between London and the coast. The 'Devon', 'Bournemouth', 'Brighton' and 'Thanet' Belles were conjoined in a poster headed 'The Four Belles Ring The South Coast', a triumph of pun over geometry.

But the mainstay of this new publicity drive was display advertising, and because of improved techniques in lithographic printing, enabling detailed work to be reproduced with great precision, there began what J. T. Shackleton, in his book of the same name, has called 'The Golden Age Of The Railway Poster'. The largely prosaic pre-war approach was replaced by more creative and imaginative content. Frank Pick at London Transport pioneered the use of striking and memorable artwork in the service of a corporate image, and both LNER and GWR were influenced by the 'modern' approach when they adopted new sans-serif type-faces on their publicity. Out went words like 'breezy' and 'bracing' which too accurately described the realities of a British holiday and in came the sun. The Southern Railway forged ahead with the extrovert if unsophisticated 'Summer in the South' campaign. A ruddy-cheeked guard called Sunny South Sam (looking not unlike

John Hassall's prancing fisherman) beamed down from the posters beckoning punters to the Sunshine Coast and spraying them with sibilants in the process . . . 'Summer Comes Soonest In The South' . . . 'The Sun Shines Most On The Southern Coast' and so on. The LNER, never one for vulgarity, had been making do with the relatively uncatchy 'Drier Side Of Britain' but now it was stung into response and after some thought produced the judiciously restrained 'Meet The Sun' campaign, which hinted at some sort of solar appointments system. If your preferences were occidental you could 'Go Great Western!', where more alliteration awaited you in 'Smiling Somerset', or more specifically in Weston-Super-Mare – 'The Smile in Smiling Somerset'. For those so inclined there was Health in the Air at Aberyswyth, Natural Beauty in The Isles of Scilly and Ideal Bathing at St Ives, whilst Cornwall, never the home of understatement, became, for a short while, The Arcadian Coast.

The LNER once again tried to join in the hype, and once again proved it wasn't their game. 'Attractive Clyde Coast Resort' was all they could find to say about Helensburgh, though the poster looks very handsome, and 'Scarborough, Queen Of Watering Places' was one of those awkward half slogan, half factually-descriptive handles that the *National Geographic* magazine does so well, like 'Paris . . . Historic City on The Seine' and 'Machu Picchu – Lofty Lost City of The Majestic Andes'. However, it must be said in the LNER's favour that it was they who coined one of the most enduring slogans – 'It's Quicker By Rail'.

With the outbreak of the Second World War this burst of creative marketing energy not only skidded to a halt, it was thrust hastily into reverse. The message now was not to get people on trains but to get them off. The only slogan that really mattered was 'Is Your Journey Really Necessary?' When peace came in 1945 it was clear that the railways would never be the same again. Exhausted by the strain on machines and workforce and starved of the investment needed to rebuild the system, the private companies could mount no coherent opposition to nationalisation, and in 1947 the Great Western,

Fast food of a bygone age: a 1928 GWR Catering Basket, with monogrammed tea set, fruit cake and individually doillied slices of bread.

The Quick Lunch Bar, Paddington, 1936, an Art Deco interior misleadingly reminiscent of a New York diner.

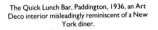

The Torbay Express, perhaps conveying happy holidaymakers to 'Paignton – The Family Resort of Picturesque Torbay'.

the London and North Eastern, the London Midland and Scottish, and the Southern Railway companies became plain British Railways. Austerity and economy reached every corner of the enterprise and advertising was no exception. 'Travel By Train', 'See Britain By Train' were the plain, functional exhortations which seemed to suit the times, as did the choice of poster subjects. Beautiful Wales, Olde England, The Heritage Series were sober reminders of the good and lasting things about a country that was undergoing such a traumatic period of social and economic change. The landscapes and the architectural scenes produced in the 1940s and 1950s by the likes of Jack Merriott, Claude Buckle and Frank Sherwin are full of meticulous detail and in the case of Lichfield Cathedral (unattributed) the effects of light and shade are reminiscent of the seventeenth-century Dutch painters. The aim of these later poster painters was to encourage the traveller to the lesser-known corners of the country – the Eden Valley, the villages of Cambridgeshire, Loch Eck, all of which could then still be reached by the railway.

They were the last of the good·days, when Dr Beeching's Re-shaping Report (advocating the closure of 5000 miles of track and 2350 stations) was as remote as the past whose monuments the artists were so carefully representing.

All the posters in this collection are evocative in their own way, and one or two I dwell on particularly – Frank Mason's view of London, painted in 1946, and issued in the GWR's last year of existence, is quite a rarity, one of the few holiday posters which depicts railway activity, or indeed machines of any sort. 'Broadstairs' shows us a lesser monument, the Great British Sandcastle, flanked by The World's Most Attractive Family. Not a grain of sand adheres to these handsome folk as the future Richard Rogers tops out his building, whilst his adoring sister pats the car park area. Further round the coast, Bognor Regis is clearly aiming for the singles market with a tall, slim, raven-haired voluptuary practising long throw-ins from an azure sea. In Paignton – Family Resort of Picturesque Torbay – the artist dithers between glamour and geology, with pleasantly erotic results.

It's axiomatic in these posters that the beaches, beside being made up of non-stick sand, are never as crowded as they are in real life, but in the GWR/LMS joint 'Weston-Super-Mare' poster the beach is a rich brown smudge as empty as if an epidemic had hit it, whilst the romance blossoming in left foreground makes you almost want to cry out loud and warn the girl. The two Royal Leamington Spa posters provide an interesting contrast in styles. Jack Merriott's church and street scene for British Railways is safe and somewhat unambitious, whereas Ronald Lampitt's poster, for

Demob-suited man, young mother and war baby at Southend: a *Picture Post* celebration of the return to Britain's coastal resorts in 1945.

GWR, uses a bolder more eye-catching approach. If his brief was to sell the waters he's succeeded magnificently. It looks like a more stylish precursor of the Badedas series and should be captioned 'Things Happen After A Glass Of Water In Leamington Spa'. Another eye-catching poster by one of the most original artists of 'The Golden Age' is Tom Purvis's Robin Hood's Bay. Purvis worked mainly for the LNER for whom he produced an elegant series called North East Joys (reproductions of which are available at the National Railway Museum in York). His use of colour, line and perspective is refreshingly imaginative and an example of what a good poster should do – convey a clear, uncluttered, attractive image. The Holiday Runabout and the Butlin's poster, are set firmly in the post-war period, and show the nature of holidays diverging, on the one hand the get-away touring holiday and on the other the stay-together holiday camp. The word 'Runabout' is an early instance of the compression of language and the growth of 'Adspeak', as surely a sign of the future of advertising as 'Shrewsbury – Historic

Centre Of A Most Beautiful County' was of the past.

Curiously enough, though, we seem to be going through one of those aesthetic cycles in which decorative artwork and richer, more experimental graphic design is returning after the functionalism of the late 1960s and 1970s. Though the railways no longer offer the rich potential of subjects and destinations reflected in this collection, there are definite signs of a revival in striking and colourful poster design and of a regard for the period when railways were seen as friendly, reassuring and irreplaceable elements in the enjoyment of the British countryside. We seem to have more in common with the 1920s and 1930s than we do with the 1960s and 1970s. We want diversion, fun, style, colour. We want some of the dream back.

What we can never have back is the dominance of the poster as a means of advertising, as it takes its place in a market saturated by television advertising and videos. With television has come market research, the honing down, clarification and identification of a potential audience in a way which was impossible in the inter-war years. Yet the techniques of deception remain the same – exaggeration, omission, selectivity. Look at almost any motor car advertisement these days and see how much, if any, relationship it bears to everyday

The organized holiday: orderly luggage awaits
the coach for the train home. Butlin's Holiday
Camp, Filey, 1946.

Fun in the sun – a beauty contest at Butlin's,
Skegness (surely the man at the end doesn't
expect to get away with it?).

driving conditions. Similarly, with no apparent aware-
ness of the irony, packaged and processed foods are sold
by cleverly evoking and extolling the world before packaged and processed foods existed.

A few years ago, whilst filming a holiday story for the
BBC set in Suffolk of the 1950s we sat around one day
trying to devise slogans for the Suffolk Coast. The one I
liked best was in the finest alliterative traditions of
Sunny Sam and Smiling Somerset but somehow I doubt
it would ever be used, 'Suffolk . . . Sun, Sea and Sizewell
B!' We may think we are a lot more sophisticated in our
advertising nowadays, but we're still happy to be told
stories if it makes us feel better . . . And that's what
these posters are all about.

MICHAEL PALIN

I would like to acknowledge the help of the following:
G. Freeman Allen *Railways In Britain* (Marshall Caven-
dish Ltd, 1979)
Anthony Hern *The Seaside Holiday* (Cresset Press, 1967)
J. T. Shackleton *The Golden Age Of The Railway Poster*
(New English Library, 1976)
Roger Burdett Wilson '*Go Great Western*' (David and
Charles, 1970)
*Posters Of The Yorkshire Coast: An exhibition orga-
nised by Ferns Art Gallery, Hull and the Museum and
Art Gallery Service for Yorkshire and Humberside*
(Text by Jennifer A. Rennie, 1980)
'*It's Quicker By Rail!*' Exhibition of Railway Posters at the
National Railway Museum, York, 1987.
My colleagues at Transport 2000, Alison Davies at
Mayday Management, and especially Geoff Body of
Avon Anglia Publications and Services, who was an
invaluable source of information.
The very helpful staff at the library, National Railway
Museum, York. Judith Wilson and Colin Webb at
Pavilion for their unswerving, nay untilting support.

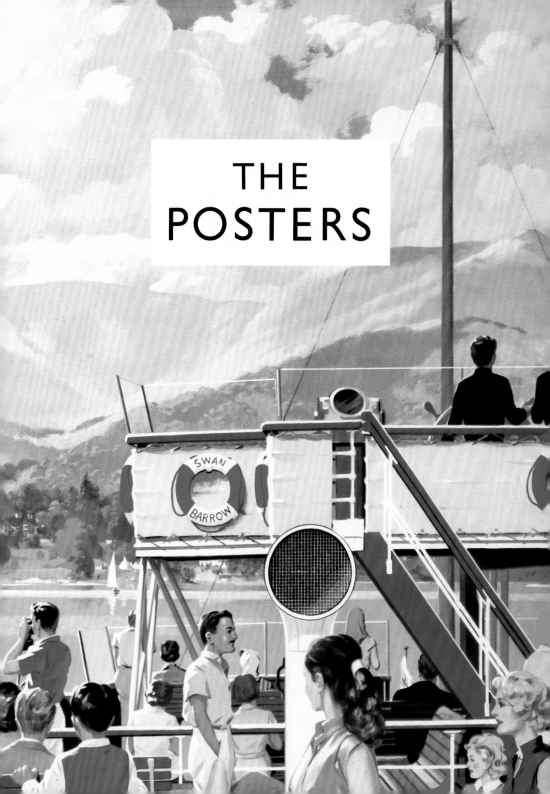

THE
POSTERS

Interesting because of its date, 1947, the last year of existence for the Great Western Railway who commissioned it, and also because it is one of the very few posters in this selection which portrays not escapist peace and tranquillity but the hustle and bustle of people on the move. A very fine composition by Frank Mason, combining past and present successfully. Note for bridgophiles: the condition of Blackfriars Bridge is as colourful and well painted as its present-day restoration despite being just after the War. Note for poets: who is Davidson?

ST PAULS.   FRANK H MASON 1935

LONDON GWR

"Afloat upon ethereal tides
St. Paul's above the city rides"

Davidson

HAPPY HOLIDAYS

Windsor Castle and the River Thames, one of the most potent
and enduring images of England, given a light invigorating flavour
of summer by Frank Sherwin. Sunshades, boats, swans and the
huge looming trees that border the river capture the character
of the Thames Valley and temptingly convey the pleasures of the
combined rail and river trips which were such good business for
British Railways.

FRANK
SHERWIN

WINDSOR

SPECIAL FACILITIES AVAILABLE FROM LONDON AND MANY OTHER STATIONS
CIRCULAR RAIL—RIVER TRIPS WITH ATTRACTIVE CONDUCTED TOUR
DURING THE SUMMER MONTHS

TRAVEL BY TRAIN   BRITISH RAILWAYS

PUBLISHED BY BRITISH RAILWAYS (WESTERN REGION) P.X. 56   PRINTED IN GREAT BRITAIN BY JORDISON & CO. LTD. LONDON AND MIDDLESBROUGH

HAPPY HOLIDAYS

One of the Southern Region's 1950s 'modern' posters, extolling the 'fast electric trains' from London to the Kent coast. Not much to see of Broadstairs, the artist is more concerned to present the idealized British family of the 1950s. Perhaps mum is a little too glamorous, but dad is as solid as the cliff behind him, smoking his pipe with pride.

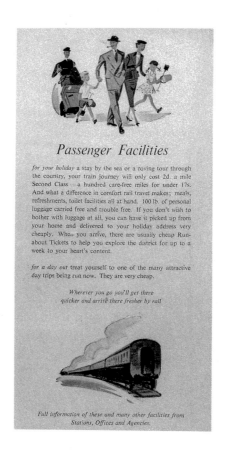

Passenger Facilities

for your holiday a stay by the sea or a roving tour through the country, your train journey will only cost 2d. a mile Second Class — a hundred care-free miles for under 17s. And what a difference in comfort rail travel makes; meals, refreshments, toilet facilities all at hand. 100 lb. of personal luggage carried free and trouble free. If you don't wish to bother with luggage at all, you can have it picked up from your home and delivered to your holiday address very cheaply. When you arrive, there are usually cheap Runabout Tickets to help you explore the district for up to a week to your heart's content.

for a day out treat yourself to one of the many attractive day trips being run now. They are very cheap.

*Wherever you go you'll get there
quicker and arrive there fresher by rail*

*Full information of these and many other facilities from
Stations, Offices and Agencies.*

Broadstairs

HOURLY SERVICE OF FAST ELECTRIC TRAINS FROM LONDON

Guide (9d. P.O.) from Information Bureau, Dept. R.P., Broadstairs, Kent

SOUTHERN

BRITISH RAILWAYS

HAPPY HOLIDAYS

Alan Durman's energetic and eye-catching portrayal of a woman with a fluorescent body is one of the few posters here in the 'modern' style. Anticipating the advertising styles of the 1960s and 1970s, Durman goes for a single strong image rather than a lot of visual information. As the surf breaks around the sturdy thighs of this ball-playing goddess one thing is clear. Bognor is a singles town.

BOGNOR REGIS

Frequent electric trains from London (Victoria)

BRITISH RAILWAYS

ILLUSTRATED GUIDE (6ᵈ) FROM PUBLICITY DEPT. TOWN HALL BOGNOR REGIS. SUSSEX

PUBLISHED BY BRITISH RAILWAYS (SOUTHERN REGION) AD 4441/825   PRINTED IN GREAT BRITAIN BY LEONARD RIPLEY & CO. LTD., VAUXHALL, LONDON

Leonard Richmond's 1930s poster for Jersey makes the island seem very empty and attractive. He's also honest; rocks weren't normally allowed to mar idyllically golden beaches and one feels his colouring is much more like the real thing than the idealised versions presented by his fellow artists.

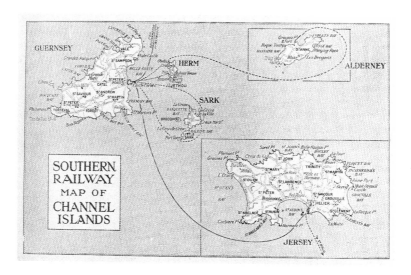

SOUTHERN
RAILWAY
MAP OF
CHANNEL
ISLANDS

JERSEY
SUNSHINE · SANDS · SCENERY

SOUTHERN RAILWAY   **GREAT WESTERN RAILWAY**
via **SOUTHAMPTON**   via **WEYMOUTH**
DAILY SERVICES by JERSEY AIRWAYS
Guide Free from Town Clerk. Jersey.

The Great Western and Southern are both mentioned here, suggesting that the Guernsey authorities were the initiators of this poster. Though the man in the foreground is chiefly remarkable for the enormity of his trousers, the girl's hair, scarf and dress suggest a cooling breeze on the cliff top vantage point from which the artist presents us with a plethora of holiday possibilities.

GUERNSEY
THE SUNSHINE ISLAND
SERVICES VIA WEYMOUTH OR SOUTHAMPTON
BY GREAT WESTERN OR SOUTHERN RAILWAYS

FOR OFFICIAL HANDBOOKS SEND 3D TO PUBLICITY MANAGER, STATES OFFICE, GUERNSEY

PRINTED IN GREAT BRITAIN

1950s modern again. A single bold holiday image – in this case the deckchair – replacing the often tedious pictorial approach. A new up-to-date typeface and emphasis on the family once again.

Here, D. L. Mays achieves a satisfying series of sweeping lines and curves which cover a spectacular amount of the Torbay coastline whilst still creating a strong unified visual impact. The girl is awfully near the edge of the cliff.

PAIGNTON SOUTH DEVON

THE FAMILY RESORT OF PICTURESQUE TORBAY

Guide 6d. from Dept. "P", Publicity Manager, Paignton

TRAVEL BY TRAIN

BRITISH RAILWAYS

PUBLISHED BY THE RAILWAY EXECUTIVE (WESTERN REGION) P.R. 19   PRINTED IN GREAT BRITAIN BY JORDISON & CO. LTD., LONDON AND MIDDLESBROUGH

Always heavily advertised as somewhere rather special, at times a 'Riviera', at others 'The Arcadian Coast', Cornwall is here recommended, rather riskily I would think, as being available Any Day by Any Train, Anywhere. This bright attractive freshly colourful poster amalgamates the quieter attractions of the Royal Duchy – old crafts, steep cobbled streets, rocky headlands and sturdy old cottages. But by the empty look of the streets the advertising isn't working.

CORNWALL

MONTHLY RETURN TICKETS **ANY DAY ANY TRAIN ANYWHERE**

No. 185. PADDINGTON STATION, W.2.   PRINTED IN GREAT BRITAIN BY JORDISON & CO., LTD., LONDON AND MIDDLESBROUGH.   JAMES MILNE, GENERAL MANAGER.

Quite a difficult brief this one. How would *you* draw the Isles of Scilly? John S. Smith's solution is to go as far up the hill as possible and try to get the lot in. The result is a fine study of the RMV *Scillonian* slipping harbour toward a lot of unspecific grey lumps. A tantalising getaway image, but the weather seems to belie the first part of the slogan beneath.

REGISTERED SEATS

CORNISH RIVIERA EXPRESS

AND

TORBAY EXPRESS

Mondays to Fridays inclusive
11th June to 14th September, 1956

Passengers travelling on the following trains are required to hold Registered Seat Tickets in addition to Rail Travel Tickets

10.30 A.M.	PADDINGTON TO PENZANCE AND WEYMOUTH	REGISTERED SEAT TICKET HOLDERS ONLY FROM PADDINGTON
12.00 NOON	PADDINGTON TO KINGSWEAR	
11.25 A.M.	KINGSWEAR TO PADDINGTON	REGISTERED SEAT TICKET HOLDERS ONLY

- Limited accommodation
- All seats on these trains bookable in advance
- Reservations are limited to the total seating capacity of the trains
- When booking Registered Seats, rail travel tickets must be produced
- Registered Seat fee 1/- per seat, First or Second class
- Reservations may be made at Stations, Offices and Agencies

ADVANCE BOOKING ESSENTIAL

Full details from Stations, Offices and Agencies

BRITISH RAILWAYS

THE
ISLES OF SCILLY

FOR SUNSHINE AND NATURAL BEAUTY

TRAVEL BY RAIL TO PENZANCE, THENCE
BY BOAT, R.M.V. "SCILLONIAN", TO ST. MARY'S

ACCOMMODATION ENQUIRIES
TO THE CLERK OF THE COUNCIL (DEPT. 'P')

BRITISH RAILWAYS

PUBLISHED BY BRITISH RAILWAYS (WESTERN REGION) P.R. 99.   PRINTED IN GREAT BRITAIN BY CHARLES & READ LTD., LONDON & HARLOW.

A luminous almost dream-like light from a setting sun suffuses this view of the harbour at St Ives by Herbert Truman. The old-timer at one side and the young girl at the other frame the foreground in an oddly touching combination. An unusual and original composition, full of character.

Herbert Truman

ST. IVES · CORNWALL
CARBIS BAY & LELANT
GLORIOUS · IDEAL ·
· SANDS · BATHING

BOROUGH OF · 1639 · SAINT IVES

Nº 187.   Guide free (Postage 2½d.) on application to Mr. G. Carrick, Information Bureau, St. Ives, Cornwall.   PRINTED IN GREAT BRITAIN BY BECK—INCHBOLD—LEEDS

HAPPY HOLIDAYS

Commissioned by British Railways' Western Region in 1948, but the scene might have been any time in the last 300 years. Timelessness, security, peace and harmony. Thatched roofs and church towers. Ideal England, without a station in sight.

SOMERSET

Travel by Rail

Henry Riley's holiday-makers from Barmouth (q.v.) turn up again in Weston-Super-Mare. Mum has just had her hair done and Johnny is raring to go with his bucket and spade. Riley seems to have captured the second after a photo has been taken. Behind them Weston is full of happy people desporting themselves along elegant promenades, unaware of Greenpeace or the problems of untreated sewage.

WESTON-SUPER-MARE

THE SMILE IN SMILING SOMERSET

Guide free from A. R. Turner, Town Hall, Weston-super-Mare

TRAVEL BY TRAIN

PUBLISHED BY THE RAILWAY EXECUTIVE RAILWAYS APP.RY. XE 44   PRINTED IN GREAT BRITAIN BY HERISON & SON, LTD., LONDON AND MIDDLESBROUGH

Was Claude Buckle bored with landscapes? He always seems to spice up his views with a bit of human action in the foreground, and this is no exception. Very probably some local subcommittee would have decreed how they wanted their borough depicted, and Buckle, having made Weston-super-Mare look like the Côte D'Azur cannot resist a hint of 'Tender Is The Night' action in the left foreground.

WESTON
SUPER - MARE

 in Smiling Somerset LMS

Guide FREE from A.R.Turner, Town Hall, Weston Super-Mare

HAPPY HOLIDAYS

A powerful piece of foreshortened perspective from Claude
Buckle gives a striking, if idealized, view of the Avon Gorge,
capped with one of the masterpieces of nineteenth century
engineering, the Clifton Suspension Bridge. It is ironic that this
road bridge should have been the great railway engineer
Isambard Brunel's favourite project. 'My first child, my darling' he
once called it.

42
60
74

BRISTOL

Booklet from City Information Bureau, The Centre, Bristol I.

TRAVEL BY TRAIN

PUBLISHED BY THE RAILWAY EXECUTIVE (WESTERN REGION) WE. 331

PRINTED IN GREAT BRITAIN BY JORDISON & CO. LTD., LONDON AND MIDDLESBROUGH

Lander's poster, originally produced for the Great Western Railway but much repeated later, uses an eye-catching collage to give Ross-on-Wye an image of solid reticence, very different from the seaside atmospheres. Rich blocks of autumnal colours stacked up above the river capture quite accurately my own memory of Ross. Leafy and retiring. By framing the collection of facades old and new with trees and woodland, Lander rather cleverly combines Ross's domestic charms with a hint of the wilder, more wooded attractions of the valley beyond.

Now

Get about with a holiday runabout ticket

Ask at the station

Lander

ROSS-ON-WYE

THE GATEWAY OF THE WYE

Information and Accommodation List from
The Secretary, Chamber of Commerce, Ross-on-Wye

WESTERN (BRITISH RAILWAYS) REGION

P.W.26 PUBLISHED BY THE RAILWAY EXECUTIVE (WESTERN REGION)   PRINTED IN GREAT BRITAIN   BECK & INCHBOLD   LEEDS

HAPPY HOLIDAYS

Another of the prolific Jack Merriott's street scenes. This was, surprisingly, issued by BR's North Eastern Region. Though the likelihood of persuading people from Middlesbrough to do a day's shopping in Hereford seems remote, it has a rather pleasing harmonious mediaeval feel to it. As in much of the post-Second World War railway advertising the intention seemed to be to show how little things had changed.

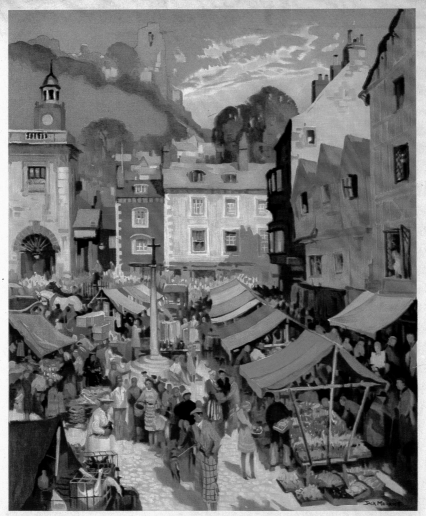

MARKET DAY

CHEAP DAY TICKETS
TO
HEREFORD
EACH WEDNESDAY
FROM THIS STATION

PUBLISHED BY THE RAILWAY EXECUTIVE (NORTH EASTERN REGION)   PRINTED IN GREAT BRITAIN   WATERLOW & SONS LTD. LONDON & DUNSTABLE

The sun setting behind misty mountains and the outlines of trees in the foreground give this a formality of style and pattern which is quite distinguished, a touch oriental, and gives an air of mystery and elegance to this mid-Wales town not previously known as one of the hot spots.

Llandrindod Wells

THE WYE VALLEY
HEALTH & HOLIDAY RESORT

Illustrated Guide on application to Secretary Dept. B.R., Information Bureau

TRAVEL BY TRAIN

BRITISH RAILWAYS

HAPPY HOLIDAYS

The prolific Jack Merriott in rather wistful style. The slogan 'There's Health In The Air' is a 1950s variation on the Victorian preoccupation with ozone and the Edwardian quest for 'bracing climates'. The healthy sea air is an enduring and potent myth.

ABERYSTWYTH

There's health in the air and a friendly sun

TRAVEL BY TRAIN

BRITISH RAILWAYS

HAPPY HOLIDAYS

Nice to see people, as well as scenery, in this archetypal 1950s
holiday poster by Henry Riley. Issued in 1956 it could well be
retitled 'Happy Families'. In this panorama of beach activities
everyone is doing something decent, no one is moping, yelling or
kicking sand in anyone else's face, whilst the golden sands and
gentle blue waves are reflected in the protective presence of
Cader Idris in the east. The splendid half mile long railway viaduct
into Barmouth is not included, however.

40

BARMOUTH NORTH WALES

FOR MOUNTAIN, SAND & SEA

Illustrated Guide 6d., Heulwen Tourist Office, Barmouth

TRAVEL BY TRAIN

PUBLISHED BY BRITISH RAILWAYS (WESTERN REGION). P.R.86-56/57

PRINTED IN GREAT BRITAIN BY JORDISON CO. LTD., LONDON AND MIDDLESBROUGH

Sydney Lee experiments here with a swirling expressionist style to capture Snowdon in an original and interesting way. The commissioning company, the LMS, were not sure about it at first. Lee was best known as an etcher and wood engraver.

London Midland and Scottish Railway Company.

NOTICE

Well-appointed Bath and Dressing Rooms are provided as follows :—

LONDON (Euston—No. 6 Platform).

    ,,   (St. Pancras—No. 2 Platform).

MODERATE CHARGES.

SNOWDON
from Llyn Llydaw
NORTH WALES
LONDON MIDLAND & SCOTTISH RAILWAY

HAPPY HOLIDAYS

An unusual poster in that it contains, sensibly, a map of its route,
and because it includes the railway and the earliest diesel railcars,
then exciting and innovative enough to be added to the
landscape. Frank Wootton, well known for his interest in
depicting cloud formations, is the artist.

NEAR LLANRWST

THE CONWAY VALLEY

Enjoy the lovely North Wales scenery
from one of the new Diesel Trains

Faster – Cleaner – More Comfortable –

Painted by Claude Buckle, this Stratford street scene seems aimed at the American market, with British and US flags adorning the half-timbering and much made of the Garrick Inn and Harvard House signs. A liaison of some sort is going on in the right-hand foreground. Anglo-American relations?

STRATFORD
ON-AVON

TRAVEL BY RAIL   BRITISH RAILWAYS

PUBLISHED BY THE RAILWAY EXECUTIVE (WESTERN REGION) PW 41   PRINTED IN GREAT BRITAIN BY WATERLOW & SONS LTD, LONDON & DUNSTABLE

HAPPY HOLIDAYS

'Things Happen After A Glass Of Water At Leamington Spa'.
This GWR poster by Ronald Lampitt, besides giving a Marienbad
look to Leamington Spa, is as bold and eye-catching as a good
poster should be, another example of the experimental graphic
techniques encouraged by the private railway companies in the
1930s as compared to the more staid approach of British
Railways in the 1950s.

HOLIDAY SEASON TICKETS

afford the most economical travel
facility for completely exploring
your holiday district.

Unlimited journeys by RAIL over
an extensive area

FOR ONE WEEK

10/6 **15/9**

THIRD CLASS   FIRST CLASS

WEEKLY TICKETS IN THE
SAME AREAS FOR

DOGS - 2/8
CYCLES - 5/3

It will pay you to
Enquire at your destination station for details

HOLIDAY SEASON TICKETS are issued in

CORNWALL	WEST WALES	THE MALVERNS
DEVON	CAMBRIAN COAST	THE COTSWOLDS
SOMERSET	DEE VALLEY	SHAKESPEARE
DORSET	WYE VALLEY	COUNTRY, etc., etc.

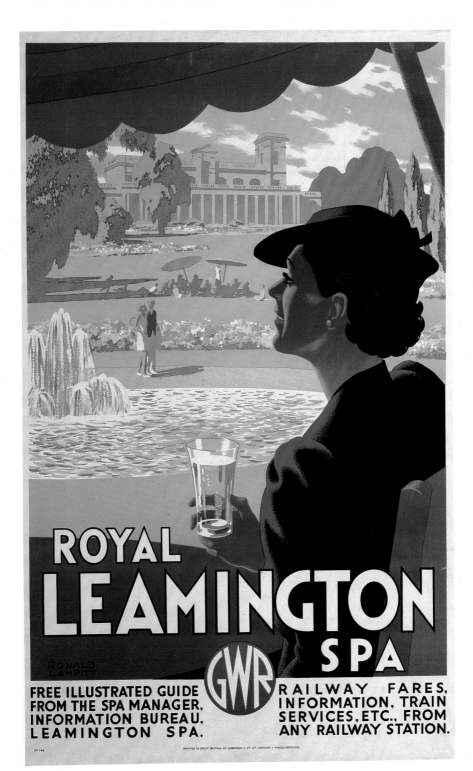

HAPPY HOLIDAYS

One feels that today's sophisticated media manipulators would
have had little time for a poster depicting a road in Leamington
Spa, but Jack Merriott's worthy if insipid study does capture the
respectability of the place. The message is discreetly but
unmistakably clear: no riff-raff in Royal Leamington Spa.

ROYAL

LEAMINGTON SPA

TRAVEL BY TRAIN

Illustrated Guide Book (Post 6d.) from Spa Manager,
Room R, Pump Rooms, Royal Leamington Spa, Warwickshire.

WESTERN REGION

PUBLISHED BY BRITISH RAILWAYS (WESTERN REGION) P.B.V.R&L 56   PRINTED IN GREAT BRITAIN BY THE PHOTICE PRESS LTD., LONDON, S.E.5

HAPPY HOLIDAYS

Back to the 1950s. An inviting depiction of an idyllic English village in which Edward Wesson employs his sub-El Greco technique. Wicket gates, thatched roofs and overflowing gardens, with no machinery or even humanity in sight. This was part of British Railways' creditable policy of attracting travellers to less visited parts of the country.

MELBOURN

CAMBRIDGESHIRE

SEE BRITAIN BY TRAIN

PUBLISHED BY BRITISH RAILWAYS (EASTERN REGION) P.P. 1138   PRINTED IN GREAT BRITAIN   JORDISON & CO., LTD., LONDON AND MIDDLESBROUGH

HAPPY HOLIDAYS

This softly lit, beautifully drawn composition is one of my favourites among the traditional style of 1950s posters. Its quality is reminiscent of Dutch eighteenth century painting. The artist's name is Greene. The bold blotting out of half of the cathedral by a large tree adds depth and interest.

LICHFIELD CATHEDRAL
SEE BRITAIN BY TRAIN

Published by British Railways (London Midland Region)   Printed in Great Britain by Jordison & Co., Ltd., London and Middlesbrough

HAPPY HOLIDAYS

In the sober pictorial tradition of post-Second World War advertising, the emphasis here is on history, and only one modern vehicle is allowed to intrude on this attractive evocation of a breezy summer day. Shrewsbury is advertised as a 'centre', emphasizing the importance of the touring market which was expanding rapidly.

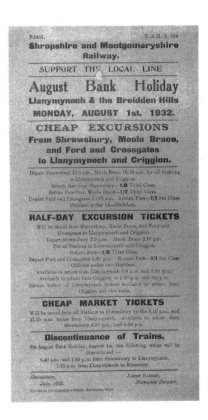

THE OLD MARKET HALL

SHREWSBURY

HISTORIC CENTRE OF A MOST BEAUTIFUL COUNTY

Free Illustrated Guide from Town Clerk, Shrewsbury

TRAVEL BY TRAIN

 BRITISH RAILWAYS

A neo-Impressionist study of Monsal Dale in Derbyshire, a popular picnic spot for Sheffielders as I remember it. This Collins poster is remarkable for having the railway included in the view. Or perhaps the others are remarkable for so consistently leaving it out. The product, in most of the posters in this book, is the destination rather than the means of getting to it. Note for pub bores: viaducts like this must have appalled 'environmentalists' when they were first built, now it's environmentalists who want to save them. And quite right too.

THE PEAK DISTRICT

BRITISH RAILWAYS

Monsal Dale in the Peak District National Park

DERBYSHIRE

See Britain by Train

BRITISH RAILWAYS

Published by British Railways (London Midland Region) L.M. 18928   Printed in Great Britain by Jordison and Co. Ltd, London and Middlesbrough

HAPPY HOLIDAYS

A swirling sky, the compressed effect of the perspective on the buildings and a smart couple in the foreground. All hallmarks of Claude Buckle's style. Chester comes across as a somewhat solid and serious city, where men wear hats and walk purposefully.

CHESTER

Painted by F. Whatley for the LMS in 1923, the first year of its existence, this is Number 34 in 'The Best Way' series. Not only does this indicate how important the poster advertising was to the newly formed companies, it also makes me desperately anxious to see the rest. This is a fine strong composition. I especially like the immaculate gentleman in the foreground helping his lady onto a rock as if they were about to be photographed by Lord Lichfield. This was produced before photolithography so all the fine detail in the poster would have had to be copied onto stone before being reproduced.

It is particularly requested that no money be paid without a bill.

L M S

REFRESHMENT CAR

SWANSEA & SHREWSBURY

TARIFF

	s	d.	
Tea or Coffee with Plate of Cold Meat, Salad, &c. Sweets, Cheese, Biscuits, &c. ...	3	6	x
Tea or Coffee with Cut Bread & Butter	0	9	
Meat Sandwiches	0	6	
Cake, per portion	0	3	
Fancy Pastries, each	0	3	
Pot of Tea or Coffee	0	6	

x   Should Tea or Coffee not be taken, a reduction of 6d. will be made.

Wines, Spirits, Bottled Beer, Mineral Waters, Cigars and Cigarettes, at usual Prices.

LMS

INGLETON
THE LAND OF WATERFALLS
NEWLY DISCOVERED CAVERNS

Guide Book free from Secretary, Advertising Association, Ingleton, or any L M S Station or office.

HAPPY HOLIDAYS

Quite how the lone fisherman got here from the station we shall
never know, but A. J. Wilson captures the essence of escapism in
this softly attractive 1950s poster commending the little-known
but very beautiful Eden Valley. Note for nostalgics: the fine
county name of Westmorland before it was subsumed by
Cumbria.

THE EDEN VALLEY
WESTMORLAND

BRITISH RAILWAYS

The Eden near Appleby — See Britain by train

In my estimation the finest poster in the collection. And the only one by the incomparable Tom Purvis who produced many more for the LNER. Robin Hood's Bay nestles at the head of a segment of ochre sand, set between cliffs of dark brown and deep green, its human activities marked by drops of red on roofs and sails. There is a hint of the mystery of the North York moors rising in shades of blue behind the town, and beyond is the sinking sun whose light creates all these rich effects. A superbly imaginative elegant and dramatic use of line and colour, worthy of comparison with the work Cassandre and other French designers were doing at the time.

ROBIN HOOD'S BAY
YORKSHIRE BY L·N·E·R

TOM PURVIS Nº 5

HAPPY HOLIDAYS

A simple, uncluttered brown study of Hadrian's Wall by L. R. Squirrell. Two hikers, a lot of desolation and some sheep, but details below indicate that high international hopes were pinned on this poster.

THE ROMAN WALL

NORTHUMBERLAND

INFORMATION FROM PRINCIPAL TRAVEL AGENTS
OR BRITISH RAILWAYS OFFICES
NEW YORK, CHICAGO, LOS ANGELES AND TORONTO

PUBLISHED BY BRITISH RAILWAYS (NORTH EASTERN REGION) (1955)   PRINTED IN GREAT BRITAIN   JORDISON & CO. LTD. LONDON AND MIDDLESBROUGH

Reginald Mayes' poster is a reminder that even in the years of austerity after the Second World War, a Pullman service was still available, but with none of the flourishes that distinguished LNER services on the same route in the 1930s – hairdressing salons, on-train news vendors, record players, radios and cinema cars. The Queen of Scots did not survive the Beeching cuts but 40 years on Pullman travel is returning to the railways with a vengeance.

THE QUEEN OF SCOTS

PULLMAN-EACH WEEKDAY

(KING'S CROSS) **LONDON and GLASGOW** (QUEEN STREET)

calling in each direction at

LEEDS HARROGATE DARLINGTON NEWCASTLE EDINBURGH

BRITISH RAILWAYS

PUBLISHED BY THE RAILWAY EXECUTIVE (EASTERN REGION) (AR 3006)   PRINTED IN GREAT BRITAIN   JORDISON & CO., LTD., PRINTERS, LONDON & MIDDLESBROUGH

HAPPY HOLIDAYS

The get-away-from-it-all-but-don't-tell-anyone-else syndrome
again. This is the work of Frank Sherwin, a landscape painter who
was in his fifties when he completed this light cool glimpse of the
Highlands, refreshingly different from the heavy Victorian image
as purveyed by Landseer and others. Recreation and space are
the key elements here.

FRANK
SHERWIN

LOCH ECK
ARGYLL

ON THE ROUTE OF THE INVERARAY
AND DUNOON CIRCULAR TOUR

PUBLISHED BY BRITISH RAILWAYS (SCOTTISH REGION) S-1809   PRINTED IN GREAT BRITAIN BY HARDGATE PRESS LTD.

In the finest traditions of LNER elegance and style this poster, signed Templeton, uses a pared down, almost figurative approach to bring life and colour to what, on closer inspection, proves to be a long, exposed, bleak stretch of coast. The most attractive thing about this Clyde coast resort looks to be the hills on the other side of the river, but Templeton's clever composition transforms Helensburgh into something that at least deserves a better slogan.

HELENSBURGH

ATTRACTIVE CLYDE COAST RESORT

PLEASURE SAILINGS – TOURS – GOLF – TENNIS

Illustrated Folder from Secretary (Dept. P) Advertising Association and L·N·E·R Offices

A pastoral idyll, only a short journey across the water by ferry.
Most of the boats at this time were operated by the railways and
like buses, fleets of which they also owned, they were a
considerable source of income.

NORTHERN IRELAND

Travel by the services of
BRITISH RAILWAYS
ULSTER TRANSPORT AUTHORITY
GREAT NORTHERN RAILWAY BOARD

Published by British Railways (London Midland Region) LM 16202   Printed in Great Britain by Jordison & Co., Ltd., London and Middlesbrough

The growth of holiday camps in the late 1930s and 1940s meant a lot of business for the railways, and British Railways and Butlins worked very closely together to move the thousands who preferred to take holidays en masse. In this carefree swimming pool scene the Ava Gardner look-alike could just as well be advertising chewing gum or shampoo. Note the realistically cloudy sky.

Butlin's FOR HOLIDAYS

AYR CLACTON PWLLHELI SKEGNESS
(SCOTLAND) (ESSEX) (WALES) (LINCOLNSHIRE)

FILEY MOSNEY
(YORKSHIRE) (S. IRELAND)

Illustrated booklet free from 439 Oxford Street, London, W.I

Train services and fares from BRITISH RAILWAYS stations, offices and agencies

Arthur J. Mills is the artist responsible for this rather odd looking trio whose tortured expressions of delight and pain suggest that a Holiday Runabout Ticket has just released them from years in captivity. Apart from the fact that mother's left arm is clearly false one thing is for sure, they're not dressed for exploring.

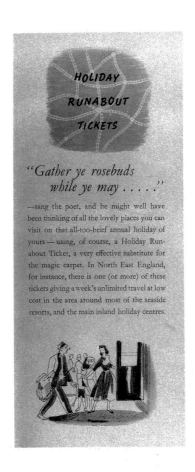

HOLIDAY

RUNABOUT

TICKETS

"Gather ye rosebuds while ye may . . . . ."

—sang the poet, and he might well have been thinking of all the lovely places you can visit on that all-too-brief annual holiday of yours — using, of course, a Holiday Runabout Ticket, a very effective substitute for the magic carpet. In North East England, for instance, there is one (or more) of these tickets giving a week's unlimited travel at low cost in the area around most of the seaside resorts, and the main inland holiday centres.

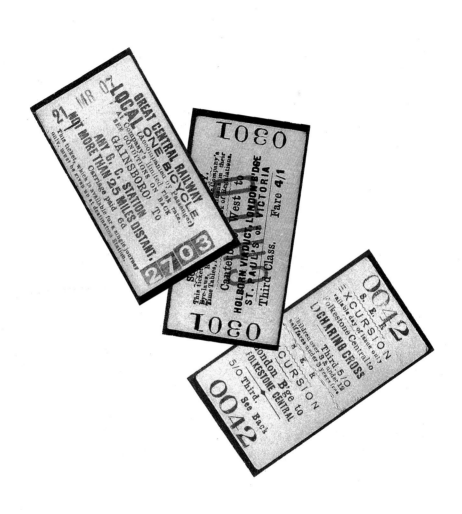